The role of literature in learning foreign languages

Xo'jayeva Sayyora Sotimboyevna

Allaberganova Umida Maqsud qizi

© Xo'jayeva Sayyora Sotimboyevna
The role of literature in learning foreign languages
By: Xo'jayeva Sayyora Sotimboyevna
       Allaberganova Umida Maqsud qizi
       Edition: June '2025
       Publisher:
Taemeer Publications LLC (Michigan, USA / Hyderabad, India)

ISBN 978-93-6908-292-6

© Xo'jayeva Sayyora Sotimboyevna

Book	:	The role of literature in learning foreign languages Our Perception of Life
Author/s	:	Xo'jayeva Sayyora Sotimboyevna Allaberganova Umida Maqsud qizi
Publisher	:	Taemeer Publications
Year	:	'2025
Pages	:	90
Title Design	:	*Taemeer Web Design*

This guide is about the benefits of literature in learning English, and it is important for teaching English to students in the 1st and 2nd stages of secondary vocational education. It can also be used by teachers, applicants, school children, and independent learners.

Editors:

Xo'jayeva Sayyora Sotimboyevna
Allaberganova Umida Maqsud qizi

Introduction

In today's era of globalization, learning foreign languages requires not only language knowledge, but also the development of skills such as intercultural communication, thinking and empathy. From this perspective, literature occupies a special place as one of the most effective tools in the language learning process. Through literary works, the reader not only acquires the language grammatically and lexically, but also gets acquainted with the values, traditions and worldviews of different peoples.

This methodological guide is dedicated to the topic "The role of literature in learning foreign languages", in which language learners will get acquainted with methods for further developing language skills - reading, writing and speaking - through literature. At the same time, important aspects such as cultural awareness and understanding other peoples are also covered.

The book aims to make language learning interesting and effective through modern teaching methods, interactive activities, creative tasks and advanced vocabulary. These materials, useful for students and teachers, allow you to learn language and culture in harmony.

This guide is intended for language learners, teachers, and any reader who wants to delve deeper into culture. Learn a language through literature — live with this language, feel it, and learn to see the world with different eyes!

LESSON 1
LITERATURE AS A TOOL FOR LANGUAGE DEVELOPMENT

Literature is a powerful resource for developing language skills. It provides exposure to real and meaningful language through various forms such as stories, poems, and plays. This authentic use of language helps learners expand their vocabulary, understand grammar in context, and enhance their overall communication abilities.

1. Wider Vocabulary

Literature introduces learners to a broad range of vocabulary in meaningful situations, making it easier to understand and remember new words.

2. Grammar in Context

Instead of teaching grammar through isolated rules, literature shows how grammar works naturally in sentences and conversations.

3. Improved Reading Skills

Reading different types of literature helps learners improve comprehension, reading fluency, and the ability to interpret and analyze texts.

4. Enhanced Writing Skills

By reading various styles of writing, learners develop their own writing abilities, learning how to express ideas clearly and creatively.

5. Better Listening and Speaking

Activities like reading aloud, acting out scenes, and group discussions help improve pronunciation, intonation, and spoken fluency.

6. Cultural Awareness

Literature reflects different cultures and societies, giving learners insights into how language connects with traditions, beliefs, and values.

7. Types of Useful Literature

Stories and Novels – Great for extended reading and deeper engagement.

Poems – Help learners focus on rhythm, tone, and expressive language.

Plays and Dramas – Ideal for speaking practice and interactive learning.

Fables and Folktales – Especially useful for young learners; they teach simple language and morals.

8. Teaching Approaches

Personal Response Approach – Learners share opinions and emotional reactions.

Language-Based Approach – Focus on vocabulary, grammar, and stylistic elements.

Literature Circles – Small group discussions that encourage collaboration and critical thinking.

In conclusion, literature is more than just reading—it's an effective, engaging, and enjoyable way to develop language skills across all areas.

COMPREHENSION QUESTIONS:
1. Why is literature considered a powerful tool for language development?
2. How does literature help learners expand their vocabulary?
3. What is the difference between learning grammar through rules and learning it through literature?
4. In what ways can literature improve reading skills?
5. How can reading literature influence a learner's writing abilities?
6. What activities connected to literature can help improve speaking and listening skills?
7. How does literature help learners understand different cultures?
8. List four types of literature mentioned in the text and explain how each one helps in language learning.
9. What are the three teaching approaches described in the text for using literature in

language development?
10. What is the overall conclusion about the role of literature in language learning?

DISCUSSION/OPINION QUESTIONS:
1. Which type of literature do you enjoy the most when learning a language? Why?
2. Do you think reading stories is more effective than doing grammar exercises? Explain your answer.
3. Can literature help in learning a second language faster? Why or why not?
4. Have you ever learned something about another culture through a book or story? What was it?
5. How would you use literature in your own language learning routine?

EXERCISES:
Exercise 1: Match the Terms
Match the teaching approach with its description:
A. Personal Response Approach
B. Language-Based Approach
C. Literature Circles
1. ___ Focuses on grammar, vocabulary, and stylistic features of the text.
2. ___ Involves students expressing their thoughts

and feelings about the literature.

3. ___ Small group discussions that encourage collaboration and critical thinking.

Exercise 2: True or False

Write True or False next to each statement.

1. Literature is only useful for reading skills, not for speaking or writing.
2. Poems help learners focus on tone, rhythm, and expression.
3. Literature does not help with cultural understanding.
4. Acting out scenes from plays can improve speaking skills.
5. Fables and folktales are especially effective for younger learners.

Exercise 3: Creative Task

Choose one of the following tasks:

1) Write a short paragraph about a book or story you've read that helped you improve your language skills.
2) Create a short dialogue based on a scene from a story or play you know and practice it with a partner.
3) Rewrite a short fable or folktale in your own words, using new vocabulary you've learned.

NEW AND INTERESTING ACTIVITIES:
1. Literary Role-Play Café
Objective: Develop speaking, listening, and improvisation skills.
How it works:
Students choose a character from a story or novel. Create a "literary café" setting where characters mingle and talk about their lives, thoughts, and decisions. Encourage students to stay in character and interact with others as if they're at a social event.
2. Quote Hunt
Objective: Improve reading comprehension and interpretation.
How it works:
Choose a literary text and pull out several key quotes. Students work in pairs or groups to find who said it, what it means, and how it reflects the theme or character. Then they present their interpretations to the class.
3. Story Remix
Objective: Encourage creative writing and vocabulary use.
How it works:

Take a short story and ask students to rewrite it from another character's point of view or change the ending.

They can also change the setting (e.g., turn a village tale into a futuristic sci-fi version).

4. Poem Performance Challenge

Objective: Practice pronunciation, intonation, and expression.

How it works:

Assign short poems or let students choose one.

They rehearse and perform the poem with expression and appropriate gestures.

Optionally, they can perform in pairs or groups and add background music or visuals.

5. Literary Instagram Post

Objective: Practice summarizing and using descriptive language.

How it works:

Students choose a scene from a book and imagine a character is posting about it on Instagram.

They create a fake post: image (drawing or digital), caption, hashtags, and comments from other characters.

6. "Hot Seat" Interview

Objective: Enhance speaking and critical thinking.

How it works:

One student sits in the "hot seat" as a character from a story.

The rest of the class asks them questions about their actions, thoughts, and feelings.

The student must answer in character.

7. Create a Soundtrack

Objective: Explore theme and mood.

How it works:

Students choose songs that fit different scenes or characters in a literary text.

They explain their choices and how the lyrics or tone match the events or emotions in the story.

LITERATURE DETECTIVE GAME PACK

Instructions for the Teacher:

- Prep: Print one envelope per group. Each envelope includes:
  - A Literary Excerpt
  - A list of Clues
  - A Mystery Statement
- Time: ~45–60 minutes total
- Groups: 3–5 students per team
- Materials Needed: Printed handouts, pens, whiteboard or chart paper (optional for scoring)

Sample Envelope (Group 1)

Literary Excerpt:
"All animals are equal, but some animals are more equal than others."
— George Orwell, Animal Farm
Clues:
1. What is the meaning of this quote?
2. What type of literary device is used here?
3. What does this say about society in the novel?
4. How does this sentence reflect irony or contradiction?

Mystery Statement:
"This quote criticizes the concept of equality as it is practiced, not as it is preached."
Task: Discuss whether this statement is true based on the excerpt and support your reasoning.

Sample Envelope (Group 2)
Literary Excerpt:
"To be, or not to be: that is the question."
— William Shakespeare, Hamlet
Clues:
1. What inner conflict does the character express here?
2. What themes are explored in this soliloquy?
3. How does the language reflect uncertainty?
4. What emotions are conveyed?

Mystery Statement:

"This line shows Hamlet's philosophical struggle with the fear of death and the unknown."

Scoring System:
Category
Points:
Correct interpretation: 1
Literary device identified: 1
Group discussion clarity: 1
Presentation (clear and logical): 1
Bonus: Strong defense in challenge round: +1

ADVANCED VOCABULARY

1. Linguistic proficiency – The ability to use language accurately and fluently in various contexts.
2. Lexical acquisition – The process of learning and internalizing new vocabulary and word meanings.
3. Narrative competence – The capacity to understand, interpret, and construct coherent and engaging stories.
4. Syntax development – The advancement of understanding and using correct grammatical sentence structures.
5. Discourse analysis – The study of how language is used in extended texts or

conversations to convey meaning.

6. Cognitive stimulation – Mental engagement that encourages learning and intellectual development, often triggered by reading complex texts.

7. Semantic richness – The depth and variety of meaning within a word, sentence, or text.

8. Idiomatic expressions – Phrases whose meanings cannot be understood from the individual words, often culturally specific (e.g., "kick the bucket").

9. Figurative language – Language that uses figures of speech like metaphors, similes, and personification to convey meaning creatively.

10. Phonological awareness – An understanding of the sound structure of language, including the ability to recognize and manipulate sounds.

11. Canonical texts – Literary works widely recognized as being exemplary or foundational in a culture or literary tradition.

12. Literary scaffolding – Using literature to support learners' language development by building on their current knowledge.

13. Genre exposure – Interaction with various literary forms (e.g., poetry, drama, fiction) to expand understanding of language and structure.

14. Character-driven narratives – Stories that focus on the psychological and emotional development of characters, which helps readers learn descriptive and emotive language.
15. Thematic immersion – Deep engagement with central themes across multiple texts, aiding in vocabulary retention and critical thinking.
16. Linguistic nuances – Subtle differences in word choice or meaning that reflect deeper understanding of the language.
17. Cultural transmission – The sharing and preservation of cultural values, norms, and history through literature.
18. Stylistic devices – Techniques used by authors to enhance expression and meaning (e.g., irony, alliteration, symbolism).
19. Language modeling – Demonstrating accurate and rich language use that learners can imitate and learn from.
20. Reading comprehension strategies – Techniques used to understand, analyze, and remember information from texts, such as summarizing, predicting, or questioning.

LESSON 2

LITERATURE AND CULTURAL UNDERSTANDING

Literature is a powerful tool for developing a deeper understanding of different cultures. Through various literary forms such as novels, poetry, and drama, readers gain exposure to the customs, beliefs, traditions, and ways of life of people from around the world. These works often mirror the cultural and historical backgrounds of the societies they represent, giving readers a window into the thoughts and behaviors of others.

Exploring literature from diverse cultures and time periods helps people become more empathetic and open to new ideas. It challenges stereotypes and promotes meaningful cross-cultural communication. For instance, experiencing the storytelling techniques of African legends, Japanese poetry, or Latin American fiction enables readers to appreciate different cultural expressions.

Moreover, literature connects people by highlighting both unique cultural traits and universal human emotions. This encourages a broader worldview and nurtures respect for cultural differences—an important skill in our globalized society.

In the context of language learning, literature also enhances vocabulary and grammar through real-life examples, while introducing learners to cultural themes, humor, and idiomatic language.

GENERAL DISCUSSION QUESTIONS
1. How does literature help us understand different cultures?
2. In what ways can literature reflect the values and traditions of a society?
3. Why is it important to read literature from different parts of the world?
4. How can reading literature reduce stereotypes and cultural misunderstandings?
5. What are some examples of literary works that have helped you learn about another culture?

ANALYTICAL/DEEPER THINKING QUESTIONS
6. How does literature act as a mirror of society and culture?
7. Can literature truly represent a whole culture accurately? Why or why not?
8. How does reading foreign literature build

empathy?
9. What role does cultural background play in interpreting literature?
10. How does literature contribute to global awareness and intercultural communication?

INTERACTIVE EXERCISE:
Discovering Culture Through Literature
Objective:
To explore how literature portrays culture and to stimulate curiosity about different traditions, customs, and worldviews.
Part 1: Cultural Storytelling Challenge
Instructions: In this section, you will immerse yourself in a short literary passage from a different culture. As a group, read the following excerpt (or provide an excerpt from a well-known culturally rich novel or short story):
> "Beneath the golden sky, the market came alive with colorful stalls, where the air was thick with the scent of spices and incense. People bargained in a language full of gestures and laughter, while children played in the alleys, chasing after stray dogs."
(This passage could be inspired by an Indian or Middle Eastern marketplace setting.)

Challenge Questions:
1. Cultural Detective:
What sensory details (smells, sounds, sights) reveal the culture of the setting? List 3 clues.
2. Visual Artist:
Create a quick sketch or doodle that represents the scene described in the text. Use symbols or colors that stand out to you based on the cultural context.
3. Cultural Insight:
In your opinion, why is the sense of community (marketplace, children playing) highlighted in this passage? What does it say about the values of the culture.

Part 2: Culture Swap – What's Similar, What's Different?

Instructions:
Think about how some cultural aspects in the passage (like the marketplace) might be reflected in your own culture. Then, compare and contrast.

ACTIVITY:
1. Culture Swap Discussion
With a partner or small group, talk about your own local marketplace or community gathering places (like a local café, park, or street fair). Write down your thoughts under the following

categories:

2. Creative Twist:

Imagine you are a character in the foreign culture's marketplace. Write a short monologue (2-3 sentences) from the perspective of a person selling goods or just walking through the market. Focus on sensory details and cultural elements you observed in the passage.

Part 3: Culture through Time – The Story of an Object

Instructions: Choose an everyday object that's important in your own culture (e.g., a piece of clothing, a dish, a tool, or a traditional instrument). Then, answer the following:

1. The Object's Story:

How would this object appear in a literary description? (Write a short, vivid paragraph about it using sensory details).

2. Cultural Symbolism:

What does this object symbolize in your culture? How does it reflect important values or customs?

3. Cross-Cultural Connection:

Do you think this object would have a similar or different meaning in another culture (e.g., a marketplace in another country)? Share your thoughts.

Part 4: Group Presentation – Cultural Showcase
Instructions:
In groups of 3–4, pick a culturally significant literary work (e.g., a novel, short story, poem, or folktale) from a culture that you haven't explored much before. Create a mini-presentation that includes:
A summary of the plot or key themes.
Cultural aspects revealed through the setting, characters, and plot.
Comparison with aspects of your own culture (based on the previous activity).
Visual aid: Use images, symbols, or props that represent the culture and literary work.
Goal:
To share insights about how literature shapes cultural understanding and to celebrate the diversity of storytelling.
Part 5: Reflect and Write – "Literature as a Bridge"
Instructions:
Write a creative response (about 5 sentences) based on the following prompt:
"After reading literature from a different culture, I feel more connected to the world because…"
Share your reflection with the class or a partner.

CREATIVE AND ENGAGING ACTIVITIES

1. Passport to Culture – Literary Travel Journal

Activity Idea:

Each student receives a "Literary Passport." Every time they read a short story, poem, or excerpt from a different culture, they "stamp" their passport.

How it works:

After reading, students write a short "travel journal entry" from the point of view of a local character in the story.

They include:

The location and culture

What they saw, felt, or experienced

What they learned about the culture

Bonus: Draw a symbol or flag representing that culture.

2. Cultural Role Play Café – "Literature Live"

Activity Idea:

Turn your classroom into an international café! Students role-play as characters from different literary works.

How it works:

Assign each group a character from a culturally diverse piece of literature.

Students research the character's background and

culture.

In a casual "café setting," they speak in role and discuss topics like food, family, beliefs, and traditions.

The twist: They can only answer based on what their literary character would say!

3. Decode the Culture – Literary Detective Game

Activity Idea:

Students play the role of "Cultural Detectives," solving clues hidden in short literary texts.

How it works:

Provide excerpts from stories or poems with rich cultural references.

Give students a worksheet with clues to find:

Traditions

Language features (idioms, greetings)

Beliefs or values

Local settings or rituals

They present their findings as a "Culture Case File."

4. Culture Through Dialogue – Literary Scene Rewrite

Activity Idea:

Students rewrite a scene from a famous literary work in a different cultural setting.

How it works:

Choose a familiar story or dialogue (e.g., from Romeo and Juliet or a folktale).

Have students reimagine it in another country or cultural context.

Change names, clothes, setting, traditions, and even dialogue.

Perform the new version as a short skit or reader's theater.

5. Global Book Trailer – Culture in 60 Seconds

Activity Idea:

Students create a short video or digital slideshow "book trailer" for a culturally rich literary piece.

How it works:

Pick a short story, folktale, or poem.

Create a 1-minute trailer that includes:

Key scenes or characters

Cultural symbols, music, or setting

A narrator's voice introducing the cultural context.

Present to the class, followed by a discussion on what the story teaches about the culture.

ADVANCED VOCABULARY LIST:

1. Intercultural – Relating to or involving two or more different cultures.

2. Narrative – A spoken or written account of

connected events; a story.

3. Allegory – A story, poem, or picture that can be interpreted to reveal a hidden meaning, typically moral or political.

4. Ethnocentrism – Evaluation of other cultures according to the standards of one's own culture.

5. Symbolism – The use of symbols to represent ideas or qualities in literature.

6. Cultural relativism – The idea that a person's beliefs and practices should be understood based on their own culture.

7. Anthropological – Relating to the study of humankind, especially their societies and customs.

8. Transcultural – Extending across or transcending cultural boundaries.

9. Diaspora – A scattered population whose origin lies in a separate geographic locale, often reflected in literature.

10. Cultural archetypes – Universal, recurring symbols or character types found across cultures.

11. Perspective – A particular attitude toward or way of regarding something; a point of view, often shaped by culture.

12. Cultural nuance – Subtle differences in meaning, expression, or sound that are culturally

specific.

13. Intertextuality – The relationship between texts, especially literary ones, and how they influence each other.

14. Sociohistorical – Concerning the social and historical context of a text or idea.

15. Multivocality – The presence of multiple voices or perspectives within a text.

16. Xenocentrism – The preference for the products, styles, or ideas of someone else's culture rather than one's own.

17. Cultural literacy – The ability to understand and participate fluently in a given culture.

18. Narrative empathy – The capacity to understand or feel what another character is experiencing through storytelling.

19. Cultural motif – A recurring theme, idea, or image in literature tied to a specific culture.

20. Cross-cultural interpretation – Analyzing a literary text by understanding its meaning through the lens of multiple cultures.

LESSON 3

THE INFLUENCE OF POETRY IN LANGUAGE LEARNING

1. Enhances Vocabulary and Grammar

Poetry introduces learners to rich and varied vocabulary, idiomatic expressions, and creative use of grammar. It exposes students to both formal and informal language, helping them understand context and connotation.

2. Improves Pronunciation and Rhythm

Because poetry often relies on rhyme and meter, it's an excellent tool for practicing pronunciation, stress, and intonation. Reading poems aloud helps learners develop fluency and natural speech rhythm.

3. Encourages Creative Thinking

Interpreting poetry requires imagination and critical thinking. It encourages students to think beyond literal meanings and explore metaphorical and symbolic language.

4. Boosts Memory and Retention

Due to its rhythmic and rhymed structure, poetry is easier to memorize than prose. Repeating poems can help reinforce language structures and vocabulary.

5. Builds Emotional and Cultural Awareness
Poetry often reflects cultural values, history, and personal emotions. Studying poetry can deepen students' understanding of the target culture and foster empathy through emotional connection.
6. Increases Motivation and Engagement
Poetry can be fun, inspiring, and emotionally resonant. When students relate to a poem, they become more engaged in learning and more motivated to explore the language.
7. Encourages Language Production
Writing their own poems gives students a chance to play with language, experiment with new vocabulary, and express themselves creatively in the target language.

COMPREHENSION QUESTIONS:
1. How does poetry help learners improve their vocabulary and grammar?
2. What makes poetry effective for practicing pronunciation and intonation?
3. Why is poetry easier to memorize compared to regular texts?
4. In what ways does poetry encourage creative thinking in language learners?
5. How can poetry help students better understand

a new culture?
6. What emotional benefits can learners gain from reading or writing poetry?
7. How does poetry make language learning more enjoyable and engaging?
8. Why is poetry a useful tool for developing critical thinking skills?
9. How does writing poetry help learners use new vocabulary and expressions?
10. What are some challenges students might face when learning a language through poetry?

EXERCISE:
Poetry and Language Skills
Objective: To explore how poetry enhances vocabulary, pronunciation, creativity, and cultural understanding.
Part 1: Vocabulary Builder
Instructions: Read the short poem below. Underline or highlight 5 new or interesting words/phrases. Use a dictionary to write their meanings.
Poem:
The moonlight whispers on the sea,
A silent song for you and me.
The breeze hums low, the stars all gleam,

Language flows like a gentle dream.
1. Word/Phrase: __ – Meaning: __
2. Word/Phrase: __ – Meaning: __
3. Word/Phrase: __ – Meaning: __
4. Word/Phrase: __ – Meaning: __
5. Word/Phrase: __ – Meaning: __

Part 2: Pronunciation Practice

Instructions: Read the poem aloud 2–3 times. Practice the rhythm and stress of each line. Record yourself if possible.

Bonus: Identify which words rhyme.

Part 3: Creative Writing

Instructions: Write a short 4-line poem in English using at least 3 new words you learned. Make it about nature, emotions, or friendship.

Example:

The morning sun begins to rise,
A golden glow in sleepy skies.
With gentle wind and peaceful light,
The world awakes from endless night.

Part 4: Reflection

Answer the question below:

How did writing or reading poetry help you understand English better?

INTERESTING AND NEW GAMES:
The Influence of Poetry in Language Learning:

1. Poetry Jigsaw

How it works:

Divide students into small groups.

Give each group a different stanza of a poem.

Each group reads, interprets, and presents their stanza.

Then, all stanzas are put together, and the full meaning of the poem is discussed.

Skills practiced: Reading comprehension, speaking, teamwork.

2. Fill-in-the-Poem (Gap-fill Activity)

How it works:

Provide students with a poem where some words are missing.

Students fill in the blanks using clues from context or a word bank.

Skills practiced: Vocabulary, grammar, contextual understanding.

3. Poem to Performance

How it works:

Students choose or are assigned a short poem.

They practice reading it with emotion, correct pronunciation, and rhythm.

Perform it in front of the class or in small groups.

Skills practiced: Pronunciation, intonation, confidence in speaking.

4. Poetry Hunt

How it works:

Prepare a classroom "hunt" with lines of different poems hidden around the room. Students move around to find them, match them with the correct titles or meanings.

Skills practiced: Reading, comprehension, movement-based learning.

5. Create a Class Poem

How it works:

Start with one line on the board: "Learning a language is like..."

Each student adds a line to build a class poem.

Read the final poem together!

Skills practiced: Creativity, collaboration, writing.

6. Poetic Translation Challenge

How it works:

Give students a short poem in English and have them translate it into their native language (or vice versa), maintaining the meaning and rhythm.

Skills practiced: Deep language understanding, cultural comparison.

7. Visualize the Poem

How it works:

After reading a poem, students draw or design an image that represents it.
Then, they explain how the picture connects to the poem's meaning.
Skills practiced: Comprehension, creative thinking, vocabulary.

A FRESH AND ORIGINAL GAME
Game Name: "Poetry Puzzle Race"
Objective: Reconstruct a scrambled poem as quickly and accurately as possible.
How to Play:
Materials Needed:
Several short poems (4–6 lines each)
Each line of the poem cut into strips and shuffled
Envelopes or small bags to hold the strips (1 poem per envelope)
Steps:
1. Divide the class into small teams (2–4 students each).
2. Give each team an envelope with the lines of a scrambled poem.
3. Teams work together to reconstruct the poem in the correct order.
4. Once they think it's correct, they raise their hands.

5. The teacher checks – if it's right, they win points or a small prize.
6. Bonus Round: Teams read the poem aloud with proper rhythm and emotion for extra points!

Learning Benefits:
Improves reading comprehension
Encourages teamwork and communication
Reinforces sentence structure and poetic flow
Practices pronunciation and speaking
Adds a competitive, fun element to poetry learning

ADVANCED VOCABULARY:
1. Prosody – The rhythm, stress, and intonation of speech, especially in poetry.
2. Alliteration – The repetition of the same consonant sounds at the beginning of words.
3. Metaphor – A figure of speech comparing two unlike things without using "like" or "as".
4. Phonemic awareness – The ability to hear, identify, and manipulate individual sounds in spoken words.
5. Lexical richness – The range and diversity of vocabulary used in a text or speech.
6. Aesthetic appreciation – Understanding and valuing the beauty and expressive power of

language.
7. Semantic depth – The multiple layers of meaning that a word or phrase can have.
8. Cognitive engagement – The mental effort and focus involved in interpreting complex texts like poetry.
9. Cultural nuance – Subtle cultural meanings or references that add depth to poetic expression.
10. Stylistic devices – Techniques used by writers to give specific effects, like enjambment, irony, or imagery.
11. Syntax manipulation – Changing typical sentence structures for artistic or expressive effect.
12. Figurative language – Language that goes beyond the literal meaning to convey complex ideas or emotions.
13. Narrative voice – The perspective or "voice" through which a poem or text is expressed.
14. Symbolism – The use of symbols to represent ideas or qualities.
15. Interpretative reading – Analyzing a text to find deeper meaning beyond the surface.

LESSON 4

DIGITAL LITERATURE AND ITS ROLE IN ENGLISH EDUCATION

1. What is Digital Literature?

Digital literature refers to literary works created and read using digital technology. This includes e-books, interactive stories, hypertext fiction, online poetry, and multimedia narratives that combine text with sound, images, video, and animation. It goes beyond just digitized print books—it involves texts designed specifically for digital platforms.

2. Benefits of Digital Literature in English Education:

Increased Engagement: Interactive and multimedia features make reading more enjoyable and captivating for students.

Accessibility: E-books and online resources are available anytime and anywhere, allowing students to read at their own pace.

Variety of Formats: Audiobooks, videos, animations, and interactive texts cater to different learning styles and needs.

Improved Literacy Skills: Digital texts often include tools like built-in dictionaries,

annotations, and quizzes, supporting vocabulary and comprehension.
Cultural Exposure: Digital platforms offer access to a global library of literature, helping students explore diverse cultures and perspectives.
3. Tools and Platforms:
E-readers and Apps: Kindle, Google Books, Audible.
Educational Websites: Project Gutenberg, CommonLit, Storybird.
Learning Management Systems: Moodle, Google Classroom (used to assign and discuss digital literature).
Multimedia Tools: Blogs, podcasts, videos, and virtual storytelling platforms.
4. Role in the Classroom:
Teachers can assign digital texts and encourage students to interact with them using highlights, notes, and discussion forums.
Students can create their own digital stories, improving writing, creativity, and digital literacy.
Group activities using collaborative platforms help build communication skills in English.
5. Challenges:
Digital Divide: Not all students have access to devices or the internet.

Distractions: Students may get distracted while using devices.

Over-Reliance: Too much screen time can affect reading stamina and focus.

6. Conclusion:

Digital literature is reshaping English education by making learning more interactive, accessible, and personalized. While there are challenges, its benefits in promoting literacy and 21st-century skills make it an essential tool in modern classrooms.

COMPREHENSION QUESTIONS
1. What is digital literature?
2. How is digital literature used in English education?
3. Name two benefits of using digital literature in the classroom.
4. What are some examples of digital literature formats?
5. How does digital literature support different learning styles?
6. What digital tools or platforms can be used to access digital literature?
7. What is one way teachers can use digital literature to improve vocabulary?

8. What challenges might students face when using digital literature?
9. Can digital literature help increase student engagement? How?
10. Do you think digital literature will replace printed books in the future? Why or why not?

An interesting and interactive exercise:

EXERCISE:
Create Your Own Digital Story
Objective: To help students understand digital literature by creating a short, interactive story using digital tools.
Instructions:
1. Choose a Theme:
Pick a simple topic (e.g., friendship, a mystery, a day at school, a fantasy world).
2. Write a Short Story (100–200 words):
Students write a short story with a beginning, middle, and end.
3. Digital Enhancement:
Use free tools like StoryJumper, Canva Story Templates, or Book Creator to:
Add images or illustrations
Include audio or voice recording
Create interactive choices (optional)

Add animations or background music (if available)

4. Presentation:

Students share their digital stories with the class or in small groups. Encourage peer feedback.

5. Reflection Questions:

What did you enjoy most about creating your digital story?

How did digital tools enhance your storytelling?

Would you rather read or create digital stories in the future? Why?

Alternative for Younger Learners or Shorter Lessons:

Have students read a short interactive digital story (e.g., from www.interactivesites.weebly.com) and answer comprehension or opinion questions afterward.

FRESH AND INTERESTING ACTIVITIES:

1. Digital Literature Scavenger Hunt

Objective: Explore different types of digital literature.

How it works:

Create a list of things students must find online (or in a shared class folder), such as:

A poem with animation

An interactive fiction story
An e-book with audio narration
A story with clickable choices
A graphic novel in digital format
Task:
Students work in pairs or small groups to find and present examples to the class.
2. Digital vs. Print Debate
Objective: Develop critical thinking and speaking skills.
How it works:
Divide the class into two teams.
Team A: Supports digital literature in education
Team B: Supports traditional print literature
Task:
Each team prepares arguments, examples, and presents in a class debate format. Allow for rebuttals and Q&A.
3. Literary Podcast Project
Objective: Strengthen speaking, reading, and analysis skills.
How it works:
Students choose a piece of digital literature (story, poem, or scene) and:
Record themselves reading it with expression
Add sound effects or music

Include a short discussion or review at the end
Tools: Audacity, Anchor, or Vocaroo.

4. QR Code Literature Wall

Objective: Promote digital reading in a fun way.

How it works:

Students find interesting short digital stories or poems and turn the links into QR codes (using free QR generators).

Print the codes and stick them on a "Literature Wall."

Classmates scan codes and read new stories every week.

5. Emoji Summary Challenge

Objective: Encourage creativity and digital expression.

How it works:

After reading a digital story, students summarize the story using only emojis.

Classmates guess what the story is about.

Then, the original student explains their emoji choices.

CREATIVE GAME:

Game Title: "Digital Lit Escape Room"

Type: Interactive group game (digital or blended)

Objective: Reinforce understanding of digital

literature through puzzles and storytelling.

Game Concept:

Students are "trapped" in a virtual library and must solve challenges related to digital literature to "escape."

Each challenge involves:
Reading short digital texts
Answering riddles or decoding messages
Completing mini-tasks using digital tools

How to Play:

1. Setup:

Create a Google Slides or Genially escape room setup with clickable tasks.

Divide the class into small groups.

2. Challenges (Sample Rounds):

Room 1: Digital Detective

Students read a digital story (link provided)
Solve a riddle hidden in the story using clues in the text format (like hyperlinks or hover text)

Room 2: Format Match-Up

Match digital literature formats to their definitions (e.g., "hypertext fiction," "audiobook," "interactive fiction")

Room 3: Decode the Genre

Watch a short animated digital poem
Solve a puzzle to identify the genre and literary

devices used

Room 4: Create & Escape

Students write a 3-sentence digital story using a tool like Storybird or Canva

Submit it to get the final "escape" password

3. Winning the Game:

The first group to complete all tasks and enter the correct final code "escapes" the digital room.

Why It Works:

Fun and competitive

Encourages deep interaction with digital literature

Involves tech tools, teamwork, and critical thinking

ADVANCED VOCABULARY:

1. Multimodal – Involving multiple methods of communication, such as text, images, audio, and video in a single work.

2. Interactivity – The degree to which users can engage with and influence a digital text or narrative.

3. Hypertextuality – The use of hyperlinks within a digital text that allow non-linear reading and navigation.

4. Augmented Reality (AR) – Technology that overlays digital information (text, images, or

sounds) onto the real world, enhancing the reading experience.

5. Digital Fluency – The ability to use digital tools creatively and effectively, especially in educational or literary contexts.

6. Transmedia Storytelling – A narrative told across multiple digital platforms and formats, such as websites, videos, and social media.

7. Gamification – The use of game elements (points, levels, challenges) in non-game settings like digital literature to increase engagement.

8. Narrative Immersion – The experience of becoming deeply mentally and emotionally involved in a digital story.

9. Accessibility – The design of digital content in a way that is usable by people with a range of abilities and disabilities.

10. Digital Pedagogy – The study and practice of teaching that incorporates digital technologies and methods to enhance learning.

LESSON 5

LITERATURE AND DEVELOPMENT OF PUBLIC SPEAKING SKILLS

1. Introduction:

Literature is not only a source of entertainment or academic study but also a powerful tool for developing public speaking skills. Through reading, analyzing, and performing literary works, students can build confidence, improve verbal expression, and enhance their ability to communicate ideas effectively.

2. How Literature Supports Public Speaking:

Exposure to Rich Language:

Literature exposes learners to a wide range of vocabulary, sentence structures, and rhetorical devices that can enrich spoken language.

Understanding of Tone and Emotion:

Reading poetry, drama, and fiction helps students interpret tone, emotion, and voice, which are essential for expressive public speaking.

Modeling Great Speeches:

Literary texts often include famous speeches, monologues, and dialogues that serve as excellent models for public speaking techniques (e.g., Shakespeare's monologues, Martin Luther King

Jr.'s speeches).

Confidence through Performance:
Activities like dramatic reading, poetry recitation, and reader's theater allow students to practice speaking in front of an audience in a structured, creative way.

3. Skills Developed:
Articulation and Pronunciation
Fluency and Pacing
Voice Projection and Modulation
Body Language and Eye Contact
Audience Engagement
Critical Thinking and Interpretation

4. Classroom Applications:
Speech Based on Literary Themes:
Students prepare and deliver speeches inspired by themes from novels, poems, or short stories.
Debates Using Literary Characters:
Role-play as characters from literature and debate moral or thematic issues.
Book Talks and Literary Presentations:
Students present summaries, analyses, or creative interpretations of literary works.
Storytelling and Oral Narratives:
Encourage students to retell or adapt literary stories in their own words.

5. Conclusion:
Integrating literature into public speaking practice provides students with meaningful content and models of powerful communication. It helps them become not only better speakers but also deeper thinkers and more empathetic individuals.

QUESTIONS:
1. How can reading literature improve your public speaking skills?
2. What types of literary works are most useful for practicing public speaking?
3. In what ways does literature help develop vocabulary and expression?
4. Why is performing a poem or monologue a good way to build speaking confidence?
5. How can analyzing a character's dialogue in a novel help with speech delivery?
6. What are some public speaking skills that can be developed through literature-based activities?
7. How can literature help a speaker better understand tone and emotion?
8. What role does dramatic reading play in public speaking training?
9. How can storytelling based on literature enhance audience engagement?

10. Do you think public speaking skills can be effectively taught through literature? Why or why not?

A creative and fresh exercise:

EXERCISE:
"Literary Speeches Reimagined"
Objective:
To improve public speaking skills by reinterpreting famous literary passages into modern, persuasive speeches.
Instructions:
1. Choose a Literary Text:
Students select a powerful passage, monologue, or dialogue from literature (e.g., Shakespeare, Jane Austen, Charles Dickens, or even contemporary novels).
2. Modernize the Message:
They rewrite the passage as a modern speech — keeping the original message or emotion but adapting it for today's world (e.g., turning Hamlet's soliloquy into a TED Talk about decision-making).
3. Public Speaking Practice:
Students rehearse and deliver their modernized speech using key public speaking techniques:

Voice modulation
Eye contact
Gestures
Pausing for effect
4. Peer Feedback:
After each performance, classmates provide constructive feedback on delivery, clarity, and engagement.
Example:
Original: "All the world's a stage…" (Shakespeare)
Reimagined Speech Title: "Life is Your Performance: Own the Stage"
Why it's Effective:
Encourages interpretation and creativity
Builds confidence in rewriting and delivering messages
Connects classic literature with real-world speaking situations

INTERESTING ACTIVITIES:
1. Character Press Conference
Activity:
Students choose a literary character and prepare to "be" that character in a mock press conference.
The rest of the class becomes reporters asking

challenging or curious questions about the character's actions, feelings, or choices.

Skills Practiced:
Improvisation, staying in role, thinking on your feet, clear articulation.

2. Literary Elevator Pitch

Activity:
Students pick a book, poem, or literary character and create a 60-second persuasive pitch to convince the audience to read it or support the character's choices.

Challenge:
They must grab attention quickly and speak with confidence — like in a real elevator pitch!

3. Story Circle with a Twist

Activity:
In a circle, one student begins telling a story inspired by a piece of literature. Every 20 seconds, another student picks up the story in the style of a different author or genre (e.g., horror, comedy, Shakespearean language).

Skills Practiced:
Creativity, tone modulation, voice control, active listening.

4. Literary Podcast Roleplay

Activity:

Students script and record a podcast episode as literary characters or authors. For example:
"Interview with Huckleberry Finn"
"Advice Show with Jane Eyre"
"Poetry Slam with Edgar Allan Poe"
Skills Practiced:
Voice expression, content organization, engaging spoken delivery.

5. Quote Transformation Challenge
Activity:
Each student draws a famous literary quote. They must:
Interpret its meaning
Create a short persuasive speech or motivational talk using it as the central message
Deliver it to the class with confidence and emotion

GAME:
Game Title: "Mic Drop Monologue Showdown"
Type: Competitive speaking & literature game
Objective: Blend literary analysis with dramatic performance and public speaking flair.
How to Play:
1. Preparation:
Each student selects or is assigned a short

monologue or speech from a literary text. They have time to rehearse, analyze tone, and add personal flair to their performance.

2. Performance Round:
One by one, students perform their monologues in front of the class.
They must deliver it like a powerful speech — using voice, emotion, gestures, and confidence.

3. Twist Challenge Rounds (Random Spinner):
After their first round, a random spinner adds a twist they must instantly adapt to in a re-performance:
Deliver it as a whisper
Pretend you're a superhero
Use dramatic pauses
Pretend you're nervous in front of a crowd
Add a modern slang twist to the same speech

4. Audience Voting:
Classmates vote for awards like:
"Best Mic Drop Moment"
"Most Dramatic Delivery"
"Best Twist Performance"
"Most Persuasive Speech"

Why It Works:
Encourages deep literary engagement
Boosts on-the-spot speaking confidence

Builds creativity, performance skills, and audience awareness

ADVANCED VOCABULARY:

1. Elocution – The skill of clear and expressive speech, especially in terms of pronunciation, articulation, and tone.
2. Rhetoric – The art of persuasive speaking or writing, often using figures of speech and effective argumentation.
3. Oratory – The art or practice of formal public speaking, especially with eloquence and power.
4. Enunciation – The act of pronouncing words clearly and distinctly while speaking.
5. Persona – The character or voice adopted by a speaker or writer, often influenced by a literary role.
6. Intonation – The rise and fall in the pitch of the voice during speech, essential for conveying meaning and emotion.
7. Cadence – The rhythmic flow of language in speech or writing, contributing to its musicality and emotional impact.
8. Allusion – A brief, indirect reference to a literary work, historical event, or cultural symbol, often used to enrich speeches.

9. Diction – A speaker's choice of words and style of expression, which affects tone and clarity.
10. Projection – The strength of speaking voice used to reach an audience clearly and confidently.

LESSON 6

THE PSYCHOLOGICAL BENEFITS OF READING ENGLISH LITERATURE

1. RELIEVES STRESS

Reading English literary works helps calm the mind and body. Getting absorbed in a story or poem can quickly reduce stress, similar to relaxing activities like music or meditation.

2. KEEPS THE MIND ACTIVE

Literature challenges the brain by requiring focus and deep thinking. This regular mental exercise can improve memory and may help prevent age-related mental decline.

3. BUILDS EMPATHY

Stories often explore different emotions and life situations. By stepping into a character's shoes, readers develop a better understanding of others' feelings and perspectives.

4. ENCOURAGES SELF-EXPLORATION

Literary texts often deal with themes such as identity, purpose, and morality. Readers may reflect on their own lives and choices while reading, helping them grow personally.

5. ENHANCES LANGUAGE ABILITY

Reading literature helps expand vocabulary and

improve grammar. It also boosts overall communication skills and strengthens confidence when using the language.

6. PROVIDES HEALTHY ESCAPE

Books offer a meaningful way to take a break from reality. Unlike passive entertainment, reading stimulates imagination and supports mental wellness.

7. INCREASES CULTURAL UNDERSTANDING

Literature introduces readers to various societies, beliefs, and historical moments. This exposure fosters open-mindedness and reduces prejudice by offering new perspectives.

QUESTIONS:
1. How does reading English literature help reduce stress and anxiety?
2. In what ways does literature keep the brain mentally active and healthy?
3. Can reading fictional characters' experiences improve a reader's empathy? How?
4. What psychological benefits can come from reflecting on the themes in literature?
5. How does reading English literature contribute to personal growth?

6. Why is reading considered a healthier escape compared to other forms of entertainment?
7. How does literature enhance vocabulary and language skills?
8. What role does English literature play in developing emotional intelligence?
9. How can reading literary works from different cultures build tolerance and understanding?
10. Do you think the psychological benefits of reading literature are as important as academic benefits? Why or why not?

An interesting and creative exercise:

EXERCISE: "A LETTER TO A CHARACTER"

Objective:
To develop empathy, self-reflection, and emotional intelligence through literature.

Instructions:
1. Choose a short story, novel, or excerpt from English literature that contains a character facing a personal or emotional challenge (e.g., Jane Eyre, The Catcher in the Rye, Of Mice and Men, or any suitable literary text).
2. Ask students to write a personal letter to one of the characters in the story. In the letter, they

should:

Show understanding of the character's emotions and situation.

Offer advice, comfort, or encouragement.

Relate the character's experience to their own life or feelings.

3. Encourage students to use descriptive language, emotional vocabulary, and thoughtful reflection.

4. After writing, students can read their letters aloud in pairs or small groups and discuss:

What emotions they connected with.

How the exercise helped them see the character (or themselves) differently.

Psychological Benefits Highlighted:

Empathy

Self-reflection

Stress relief through expression

Improved emotional intelligence

Deepened connection to literature

NEW AND CREATIVE ACTIVITIES:

1. "Literary Mood Board"

Objective:

To explore the emotional impact of literature visually and creatively.

Instructions:

Ask students to pick a book, poem, or short story that has made a significant emotional impact on them (positive or negative).

Have them create a mood board using magazine cut-outs, digital images, drawings, or words to visually represent the mood, themes, and emotions they experienced while reading the piece.

The mood board should reflect elements like colors, symbols, or scenes that captured the essence of their emotional journey with the text.

Once completed, students will present their mood boards and discuss how literature can affect emotional well-being.

2. "Empathy Mapping"

Objective:

To better understand characters' psychological states and enhance empathy.

Instructions:

Choose a character from a piece of literature that your students are familiar with.

Provide a simple Empathy Map template with four sections: "Says," "Thinks," "Does," and "Feels."

Ask students to fill in the map based on their knowledge of the character, considering the character's internal thoughts, external actions, feelings, and statements in the story.

Students will then discuss as a group how understanding these elements can help them feel more empathetic and connected to the character.

3. "Character Psychology Journals"

Objective:

To analyze the psychological development of a character throughout the story.

Instructions:

Have students select a character from a book or play they're reading.

For each chapter or section of the book, ask them to write a journal entry from the perspective of that character. The journal should explore their thoughts, fears, hopes, and psychological state at that point in the story.

Encourage students to consider how the character's experiences impact their mental health and emotional growth.

At the end of the book, students will reflect on the character's psychological evolution and how literature helps us understand human nature.

4. "Literature and Mental Health Podcast"

Objective:

To connect literature with real-life psychological

topics and raise awareness about mental health.

Instructions:

Assign students to work in groups to create a short podcast episode (5–10 minutes) where they discuss the psychological themes in a work of literature and how these relate to mental health.

The podcast should include:

A brief summary of the story.

A discussion of the character's psychological struggles.

Insights on how the literature can help readers understand their own mental health or how the character's journey mirrors common human experiences.

Encourage students to research psychological conditions (such as anxiety, depression, identity crises) and relate these to their chosen characters.

5. "The Book Therapy Session"

Objective:

To understand how literature can act as therapy for emotional healing and self-reflection.

Instructions:

In this role-playing exercise, students will pretend to be therapists who use literature as a form of therapy.

Each student selects a character from a novel who

is experiencing emotional or psychological challenges.

The "therapist" will ask the character (played by another student) questions about their problems and offer "literary therapy" using quotes, scenes, or events from the book to offer advice and healing.

The focus is on using literature to better understand personal struggles and how reading can offer solutions or solace.

6. "Literary Music Playlist"

Objective:

To connect music, emotion, and literature in a creative way.

Instructions:

Ask students to create a playlist of 5–10 songs that they believe represent the emotions or psychological themes of a book or specific character.

Students should choose songs based on how they align with the character's journey or the overall mood of the story.

After sharing their playlists, each student will explain why they chose certain songs and how those songs reflect the psychological elements of the text.

Discuss how music and literature can both influence emotional well-being and self-reflection.

NEW GAME:
Game: "Character Mindset Challenge"
Objective:
To deepen understanding of characters' psychological states and explore the emotional and mental impacts of literature.
Instructions:
1. Preparation:
Choose a set of well-known literary characters (e.g., from Pride and Prejudice, The Great Gatsby, Harry Potter, or any other texts your students are familiar with).
Write down a few psychological traits or challenges that each character faces (e.g., anxiety, self-doubt, ambition, love, etc.) on individual index cards.
Alternatively, you can create scenario cards where students have to react to a specific emotional or psychological situation a character faces (e.g., "Your character is betrayed by a friend. How do they respond emotionally?").
2. How to Play:

Split students into small teams.

Each team will pick a character from a list (or you can assign them one).

On each turn, a team will draw a psychological challenge card or scenario card related to their chosen character. They must then act out how the character would respond, using lines from the book or based on the character's mental and emotional state.

Other teams will guess the psychological trait or emotion the character is experiencing based on the performance.

After the round, the team explains why the character would act in that way, providing insights into the psychological impact of the situation.

3. Scoring:

Teams earn points for accurately identifying the character's psychological state and providing a solid explanation of the character's emotional response.

Bonus points can be awarded for creativity and how closely the acting mirrors the character's mindset.

4. Reflection:

After the game, ask students to reflect on how

literature helps us explore the psychological complexity of characters. Discuss how these activities help improve empathy and emotional understanding

Psychological Benefits:
Empathy development
Understanding of complex emotions
Enhanced emotional intelligence
Reflection on how literature affects mental health

ADVANCED VOCABULARY:
1. CATHARTIC RELEASE – The emotional release one experiences when confronting difficult or repressed emotions, often achieved through reading emotionally intense works.
2. ALTRUISM – The selfless concern for the well-being of others, often explored in literature through the characters' psychological development.
3. PERSPECTIVISM – The concept that knowledge is always influenced by personal perspective, which is shaped by the literature one reads.
4. TRAUMA PROCESSING – The psychological processing and healing of trauma, which can be facilitated by identifying with characters or events

in literature that mirror personal experiences.

5. IDENTITY FORMATION – The development of one's sense of self, which can be explored and influenced through the characters' psychological journeys in literature.

6. CATHARTIC NARRATIVE – A narrative that brings about an emotional release or relief for the reader, aiding in psychological healing.

7. INTROSPECTION – The examination of one's own thoughts and feelings, often deepened through reading literature that challenges personal beliefs or emotions.

8. PSYCHOLOGICAL RESILIENCE – The ability to recover from or adapt to difficult situations, which is often tested or depicted in literature through characters overcoming challenges.

9. DISASSOCIATION – A psychological state in which a character detaches from reality or certain emotions, often explored through complex characters in literary texts.

10. CONSCIOUSNESS RAISING – The process of increasing awareness, often through literature, about psychological and social issues that affect both individuals and communities.

LESSON 7

TEACHING LITERATURE THROUGH FILM AND MEDIA ADAPTATIONS

Teaching literature through film and media adaptations is an engaging method to help students understand and appreciate literary works. By using films, TV series, and other media adaptations of classic or contemporary texts, educators can make literature more accessible and relatable to students. This approach not only helps in understanding the plot and themes of the original literary work but also encourages critical thinking about how stories can be translated across different mediums.

1. Enhancing Comprehension and Engagement

Film and media adaptations can help students visualize complex plots, settings, and characters, making the material easier to understand. The visuals and soundtracks in movies or TV shows bring stories to life, sparking interest in the original text and increasing engagement. Students may find it easier to follow the storyline and grasp themes when they have a visual representation to support their reading.

2. Comparing Mediums

By studying the differences between a book and its film adaptation, students can develop critical thinking skills. They can analyze how the themes, character development, and key plot points are represented differently in the two mediums. For example, students can explore:
What was added or omitted in the film?
How did the filmmakers choose to represent a specific scene or character?
Why do certain elements work better in the visual medium than in literature?
This comparison teaches students to think critically about the artistic choices made in both literature and film.

3. Exploring Themes and Interpretation

Films often interpret literary works differently based on the director's vision, the actors' performances, and the cultural context of the time the adaptation is made. Discussing these differences helps students appreciate the flexibility and multiple interpretations of a story. For example, the same novel might have a very different tone or message when adapted in different time periods or cultural contexts.

4. Broadening Cultural and Historical Perspectives

Film adaptations can also help students understand the historical and cultural contexts of a literary work. For instance, watching a film adaptation of a classic novel such as Pride and Prejudice can expose students to different cultural attitudes toward gender, class, and relationships, and help them relate these ideas to the present day. Students can see how filmmakers update or reinterpret the story to resonate with contemporary audiences.

5. Developing Analytical and Reflective Skills

When students compare a literary text with its media adaptation, they practice analyzing and reflecting on the effectiveness of the adaptation. They can think critically about:

The success of the adaptation in conveying the message of the book

The emotional impact of the film versus the book

The choices made in casting, direction, and production

This encourages deep reflection on both the text and the adaptation, leading to a more nuanced understanding of the story.

6. Encouraging Different Learning Styles

Some students may struggle with reading long texts or complex literary language. Film adaptations can cater to these students by providing a more accessible way of understanding the material. It appeals to visual and auditory learners and can be an engaging way to support different learning styles while still teaching important literary concepts.

7. Bridging the Gap Between Classic and Contemporary Literature

Film adaptations can bridge the gap between older literary works and modern students. By adapting a classic piece of literature into a contemporary film or series, educators can show how timeless themes can still be relevant. It also helps students relate to stories from different time periods in a format they are familiar with, like streaming services or blockbuster films.

In summary, teaching literature through film and media adaptations is a dynamic way to engage students, encourage critical analysis, and connect literary themes with real-world applications. By comparing and contrasting the original text with its adaptation, students gain deeper insights into both the literature and the filmmaking process.

COMPREHENSION QUESTIONS:

1. How can film and media adaptations help students understand and engage with complex literary themes?
2. What are the advantages of comparing a book with its film adaptation in terms of character development and plot?
3. In what ways do film adaptations allow students to explore different cultural and historical contexts of a literary work?
4. How can analyzing the differences between a literary text and its film adaptation develop students' critical thinking skills?
5. How can teachers use film adaptations to cater to different learning styles in the classroom?

EXERCISE:

"Book vs. Movie: Compare and Contrast Debate"
Objective:
To enhance students' analytical thinking by comparing a literary work with its film adaptation and engaging in a debate about the effectiveness of the adaptation.
Instructions:
1. Choose a Literary Work and Its Film Adaptation:

Select a well-known book that has a popular film adaptation (e.g., The Great Gatsby, The Lord of the Rings, Harry Potter, Pride and Prejudice).

2. Pre-Debate Preparation:

Divide students into two groups:

Group 1 will argue that the book is superior to the movie.

Group 2 will argue that the movie is superior to the book.

3. Key Points for Discussion:

Each group should focus on several key aspects for their argument:

Plot differences: What major events were omitted or changed in the film? Did these changes affect the overall story?

Character development: How are the characters portrayed in the book compared to the film? Is there any character development that was lost or enhanced in the film?

Themes and tone: How does the film adapt the themes and tone of the book? Does it capture the essence of the original work?

Visual and sensory elements: How does the movie enhance the story through visuals, music, and special effects? Does the film interpretation match the imagination evoked by the book?

4. Debate:
After students have gathered their arguments, hold a structured debate. Each group will present their points and counter-arguments. After each presentation, the opposing team can ask questions or challenge the points made.

5. Reflection:
After the debate, ask students to reflect on the experience:

Which medium (book or movie) did they find more effective in conveying the story? Why?

How did the film adaptation change their perception of the original literary work?

What can filmmakers learn from books that might be useful for future adaptations?

Psychological Benefits:

Critical Thinking: Encourages students to analyze and compare literary and film techniques.

Empathy and Perspective: Allows students to understand different interpretations of characters and themes.

Engagement: Involves students in an active and dynamic way of learning, appealing to both visual and verbal learners.

Creativity: Encourages students to think about how stories can be adapted and retold across different media.

NEW ACTIVITIES:

1. "Adaptation Challenge: Reimagine a Classic"
Objective:
To encourage creativity and explore how literary works can be adapted for different media formats.
Instructions:
Ask students to choose a classic literary work (e.g., Wuthering Heights, Frankenstein, Moby Dick) and reimagine it in a modern setting, a different genre, or even as a different medium (e.g., a graphic novel, a YouTube series, or a podcast).
Students will create a short pitch or concept for their adaptation, explaining how the original themes and characters are maintained, what changes they've made, and why those changes are effective.
Present their ideas in small groups, and as a class, discuss the different creative choices made in the reimaginings.

2. "Scene Rewriting and Performance"
Objective:
To explore how key scenes in a book are transformed for film, and the impact of these

transformations.

Instructions:

Have students choose a specific scene from a book and its film adaptation (e.g., the ending scene in Romeo and Juliet or a climactic moment from The Hunger Games).

Ask them to rewrite that scene with a different outcome or from a different perspective (e.g., a minor character's point of view or a modernized version).

After rewriting, students will perform their version of the scene, either as a skit or through reading aloud.

Discuss the impact of the new version, how it changes the meaning of the original text, and the effectiveness of the adaptations.

3. "Soundtrack and Sound Design for Adaptations"

Objective:

To explore how sound influences the emotional and psychological experience of a film adaptation.

Instructions:

Divide students into groups and assign them a book and its film adaptation.

Ask each group to select a scene from the film

and create a new soundtrack or sound design that better reflects the emotional tone of the scene. Students can use music, sound effects, or voiceovers to match the emotions they believe are central to the scene. The focus should be on how sound influences the psychological mood or tension.

After the activity, groups will present their soundtracks and explain how they would affect the audience's emotional response compared to the original soundtrack.

4. "Literature vs. Media Adaptation: Emotional Impact Survey"

Objective:

To investigate how literature and its film adaptations affect the emotional responses of viewers/readers.

Instructions:

Have students read a short story or novel and then watch its film adaptation.

After completing both, students will fill out an emotional impact survey. The survey can include questions like:

How did the book make you feel (before, during, and after reading)?

How did the film adaptation make you feel

(before, during, and after watching)?
Did the emotional response change between the two mediums? How?
Students will discuss in groups how the emotions portrayed in the book were or weren't effectively conveyed in the film, and why the emotional response might differ between reading and watching.

5. "Directorial Choices: Behind the Camera"

Objective:

To understand the role of the director in adapting literature and how directorial choices shape the adaptation.

Instructions:

Show students a short segment of a film adaptation (e.g., a key scene from The Great Gatsby or The Lord of the Rings).

Ask students to analyze the directorial choices that were made in terms of lighting, camera angles, pacing, and casting.

Have them consider how these choices impact the story's psychological effect on the audience. For example:

How does the camera angle emphasize a character's emotional state?

How does the lighting influence the mood of the

scene?

What role does casting play in how we perceive the character's psychology?

Students can then work in groups to create a director's commentary for another scene from the same adaptation, explaining how they would handle the scene differently and why.

6. "Literary Adaptation News"

Objective:

To explore the current landscape of literary adaptations and how books are being reimagined in popular media today.

Instructions:

Assign students to research recent or upcoming literary adaptations in film, television, or other media formats (e.g., streaming series like The Witcher or Little Women).

Have them prepare a news segment (using a video, PowerPoint, or podcast) that includes:

A brief synopsis of the book and its film adaptation.

The psychological themes or emotional impact that are central to the adaptation.

A discussion on whether the adaptation stayed true to the book's themes or made changes.

Their personal opinion on the effectiveness of the

adaptation.

Present these segments to the class, and discuss the trends in current literary adaptations.

AN INNOVATIVE AND ENGAGING GAME:
Game: "Adaptation Detective"
Objective:
To test students' knowledge of both literary texts and their film adaptations, while developing their analytical and observational skills.
Instructions:
1. Preparation:
Select several well-known books and their film adaptations (e.g., The Great Gatsby, To Kill a Mockingbird, The Hobbit, The Hunger Games).
For each pair of book and movie, prepare a set of clues about the plot, characters, or specific scenes from both the book and its film adaptation. The clues should highlight key differences, such as omitted scenes, changes in character portrayal, or major plot twists.
2. Game Setup:
Divide the class into small teams.
Each team is a group of "Adaptation Detectives" tasked with solving the mystery of how a particular book was adapted into a movie.

3. How to Play:

The host (teacher) will give each team a set of clues about the book and its adaptation.

The teams will have to work together to figure out the differences between the book and the movie based on the clues provided. For example, clues could be:

"In the book, the main character has a significant internal monologue about their moral conflict. In the movie, this monologue is replaced with an intense visual sequence."

"One of the secondary characters in the book is a major character in the film adaptation."

"The film ends with a different outcome than the book, where a key event is shown in reverse order."

Teams must guess what the adaptation differences are, the purpose behind the change, and how it affects the overall psychological impact of the story.

4. Scoring:

Teams receive points for correctly identifying the differences between the book and movie and for providing thoughtful explanations of why these changes were made. For instance, did the change make the film more accessible, or did it alter the original tone of the story?

Additional points can be awarded for creative analysis of how the film adaptation affected the emotional response or themes compared to the book.

5. Final Round:

In the last round, teams can "challenge" another team by providing a clue of their own from a different adaptation, and the other team must figure it out in a limited time.

The team with the most points at the end of the game wins the title of "Adaptation Detective".

Psychological Benefits:

Analytical Thinking: Encourages students to analyze both mediums critically and observe how changes impact narrative structure and character development.

Empathy: By comparing the emotional depth of both mediums, students reflect on how literature and film elicit different psychological responses.

Collaboration: Promotes teamwork and collaborative problem-solving as students work together to decipher clues.

Engagement: The game format makes learning fun and interactive, keeping students engaged with the content.

ADVANCED VOCABULARY:
1. Intertextuality – the relationship between texts, especially how one text refers to or draws from another, often seen in adaptations.
2. Cinematic interpretation – the director's unique vision and representation of a literary work in film form.
3. Narrative fidelity – the degree to which a film stays true to the storyline and themes of the original literary text.
4. Visual symbolism – the use of imagery in film to represent ideas or themes found in the literary source.
5. Dramatic license – the freedom filmmakers take to alter or embellish aspects of a story for dramatic effect.
6. Aesthetic transformation – changes made to the artistic style or tone of a literary work when adapted into another medium.
7. Character reimagining – presenting a known literary character in a new light or form in the adaptation.
8. Cultural transposition – adapting a literary work into a different cultural or historical setting in film.
9. Medium specificity – the unique ways in which

literature and film convey meaning, emotion, and narrative.

10. Psychological resonance – the emotional and mental impact a story has on an audience, particularly when altered in adaptation.

CONTENTS:

I. LITERATURE AND LANGUAGE DEVELOPMENT
1. Introduction: The link between literature and language learning
2. Enriching vocabulary
3. Learning grammar in context
4. Developing reading skills
5. Improving writing skills
6. Enhancing listening and speaking
7. Understanding culture through literature
8. Beneficial literary genres
9. Teaching strategies
10. Conclusion: Literature as a multi-purpose tool

II. COMPREHENSION SECTION
11. Text 1: "Why Read Literature?"
12. Questions (1–5)
13. Text 2: "Books that Shaped the World"
14. Questions (6–10)
15. Text 3: "Literature and Empathy"
16. Questions (11–15)

III. DISCUSSION QUESTIONS
17. Discussion prompts (16–25)
18. Pair & group debates
19. Creative thinking questions

IV. GRAMMAR & VOCABULARY TASKS
20. Task 1: Sentence building (context grammar)
21. Task 2: Word combinations
22. Task 3: Synonyms and antonyms
23. Task 4: Collocation challenge
24. Task 5: Vocabulary in literature

V. CREATIVE WRITING AND PROJECTS
25. Writing a short story
26. Writing a literary dialogue
27. Character diary entries
28. Group writing project
29. Poem composition

VI. INTERACTIVE LITERARY ACTIVITIES
30. Literary Role-Play Café
31. Story Remix Workshop
32. Quote Hunt Game
33. Poem Performance Challenge
34. Book Cover Design
35. Hot Seat Interviews
36. Create a Soundtrack
37. Literary Timeline Game

VII. VOCABULARY BOOSTERS
38. Top 10 words: reading skills
39. Top 10 words: emotion in texts
40. Top 10 words: literary genres
41. Top 10 words: academic vocabulary

42. Vocabulary quiz

VIII. CULTURE & LITERATURE CONNECTIONS
43. Culture in fiction and poetry
44. Universal themes in world literature
45. Cultural metaphors
46. Global storytelling traditions
47. Comparing cultures through characters
48. Literature as a mirror of society

IX. CULTURAL EXERCISES AND GAMES
49. Cultural Storytelling Challenge
50. Culture Swap Activity
51. Scene Rewrite from another culture
52. Decode the Culture Game
53. Global Book Poster Project

X. REFLECTION & PRESENTATION TASKS
54. Group Presentation: Cultural Showcase
55. Reflective essay writing
56. Literature & identity
57. Personal response journals

XI. FINAL SECTION
58. Student-created Book Trailer
59. Conclusion: The role of literature in a changing world

References:

1. Lazar, G. (1993). Literature and Language Teaching: A Guide for Teachers and Trainers. Cambridge University Press.
2. Collie, J., & Slater, S. (1987). Literature in the Language Classroom: A Resource Book of Ideas and Activities. Cambridge University Press.
3. Kramsch, C. (1993). Context and Culture in Language Teaching. Oxford University Press.
4. Carter, R., & Long, M. (1991). Teaching Literature. Longman.
5. Duff, A., & Maley, A. (2007). Literature: Resource Books for Teachers. Oxford University Press.
6. Paran, A. (2006). Literature in Language Teaching and Learning. TESOL.
7. Tomlinson, B. (Ed.). (2013). Developing Materials for Language Teaching. Bloomsbury Publishing.
8. Hall, G. (2005). Literature in Language Education. Palgrave Macmillan.
9. McRae, J., & Boardman, R. (1998). Reading Between the Lines: Integrated Language and Literature Activities. Cambridge University Press.
10. Pulido, D. (2004). "The Effect of Cultural Familiarity on Reading Comprehension." The Reading Matrix, 4(3), 20–37

www.ingramcontent.com/pod-product-compliance
Lightning Source LLC
LaVergne TN
LVHW010410070526
838199LV00065B/5928